KINDS OF
SNOW

T0159396

ALSO BY SU SMALLEN

You This Close

Wild Hush

Buddha, Proof

Weight of Light

KINDS *of* SNOW

SU SMALLEN

GREEN WRITERS PRESS | *Brattleboro, Vermont*

Copyright © 2016 by Su Smallen

All rights reserved. No part of this book may be reproduced in any form or by any means, electronic or mechanical, including photocopying, recording, or by any information storage and retrieval system, without permission in writing from the publisher.

Printed in the United States

10 9 8 7 6 5 4 3 2 1

Green Writers Press is a Vermont-based publisher whose mission is to spread a message of hope and renewal through the words and images we publish. Throughout we will adhere to our commitment to preserving and protecting the natural resources of the earth. To that end, a percentage of our proceeds will be donated to environmental activist groups like 350.org. Green Writers Press gratefully acknowledges support from individual donors, friends, and readers to help support the environment and our publishing initiative.

ISBN: 978-0997452815

Giving Voice to Writers & Artists Who Will Make the World a Better Place
Green Writers Press | Brattleboro, Vermont
www.greenwriterspress.com

Cover photo of ceramic installation "From Here to There" by Kelly Connole. www.kellyconnole.com
Author photo by Anya Galli

PRINTED ON PAPER WITH PULP THAT COMES FROM FSC-CERTIFIED FORESTS, MANAGED FORESTS THAT GUARANTEE RESPONSIBLE ENVIRONMENTAL, SOCIAL, AND ECONOMIC PRACTICES BY LIGHTNING SOURCE. ALL WOOD PRODUCT COMPONENTS USED IN BLACK & WHITE, STANDARD COLOR, OR SELECT COLOR PAPERBACK BOOKS, UTILIZING EITHER CREAM OR WHITE BOOKBLOCK PAPER, THAT ARE MANUFACTURED IN THE LAVERGNE, TENNESSEE PRODUCTION CENTER ARE SUSTAINABLE FORESTRY INITIATIVE® (SFI®) CERTIFIED SOURCING

CONTENTS

I dedicate this book to

Judith Howard

with gratitude for twenty years of
her Saturday dance classes,
fields sown there,
and fields fallowed

KINDS OF
SNOW

AUTHOR'S NOTE

I have not studied trauma; trauma has studied me. I do not write, therefore, as an expert but as a participant. Trauma can take many forms. Could be death, could be love—I thought it was love. Trauma vandalized my codes and introduced translation errors. My cells failed to recognize one another.

Fight or flight.
The third adaptation, the one little spoken of, is freeze.

No longer was there a whole story. I needed the shamanic work of winter. Snow, because it conceals and erases, reveals and accumulates, gave me language. Thankfully, there are many kinds of snow.

I wrote this book in Minnesota, first in a city, in a sweet yellow house near a small lake that used to have as its point a sundial that you could walk on, but I always thought it was a compass. I would stand on that compass and face south and west, where I eventually moved, to a town surrounded by farms, in an abandoned house that had belonged to my grandparents. The House of Healing, I named it. For several winters, which now seem like one composite, time-lapsed winter, the House and I listened for snow.

PREFACE

I can't anymore tell you how it was

I remember I was cold all the time—all winter of course, and all summer too, even when, that July, it was in the nineties every day. I never warmed up. I was so unprepared.

I took notes. I talked to myself for months, voiceless, scraping my pen across lots of spiral-bound paper. At first I thought I will make poems of these, when I have released my breath from my shock-corded ribs. No—when the making of poems would be the remaking of me. This was how poems used to work.

I keep taking notes. I'm still trying to collect data. She never said why. Only 25 words. Cut. Cut. One for each year.

Problem is, I don't want to go back there. I think of Shelley Winters in *The Poseidon Adventure*; she finds the way, a long swim underwater, secures a line for the others to follow. But in leading them through she will die, and she knows it.

I am not Shelley Winters; leading you will not save your life. Even so, if it came to that, your life if I swim again through that ice-holed, cortisol-flooded year, that eternal year that began the year before, or four years before, or eleven years before, or with the first fated kiss, if it came to that, that somehow swimming through my drowned and tilted ship would save your life, then, no.

Mnemosyne, mourn me.

I had been writing about compassion and forgiveness. I had been writing about snow. And then, I knew nothing about compassion, nothing about forgiveness. It had not snowed of note for years, until today, when the spheres sang my aria, cold, without enough breath to make it through.

FIRN

We made us out of our old selves

A Memoir in Snow: First Key

What I can, I say with snow
Snow is my landscape, my scrim
My basal temperature
My score, my cloak, my closest shadow
My abacus, my incubus,
My first unlovable beloved

Three kinds of perspective
In snow
Alone in snow
Standing alone in snow
Being left
Being left standing alone in snow
Being left so having to leave my snow

BREAK

When I got the text message
I was standing in a loaner landscape
A winter beach, ocean water thrashing
Through henge rocks in dark formations
Flight and fight through 2x2 inch screens
Of primitive messaging, primitive
Receding, a blizzard of meaning
Radiating away from me,
A snowman falling to her knees

What It Means To Be Left

Someone leaves us and so we are left
Holding the traces of white stallions,
The traces of drift

WHITE PAINTINGS

A child in Prague draws who she loves with a white crayon
on white paper. She is furious because she cannot see it.
The beloved vanishes.

A woman in Rodmell writes in the dark and it is good.
In morning light she will see the pen was dry.

Rauschenberg painted 17 panels pure white to compose
his five *White Paintings*. How little color will hold
an image? How many panels will hold them all?

Before the one loss were many.
After the one, even more.
What will you make of these?
The drawing, the draft, the field.

PRISMS

The things of the air split the scene

ALL FOR NOTHING

—Nothing is not the nothing we imagine

The blue hour begins, the old snow
bright, the salmon complete their long
swim begun at dawn along the rim of the
overturned bowl. I only know how to love.
Everything I most loved spilled. Trees rise
like classifications for the cargo of being,
or not being. On watch, I pace the cages
of grief. Until it is only cold. Blue salmon.
Lambent snow. Look, look, I say to no
one and myself. Look at the grass heads,
the gravestones you circle. Look at the
sidewalk framing a red mitten reaching
toward a red ball. The blue hour deepens.
Somewhere waves stack stones, rock
rocks. The last of light drops the quickest,
into a velvet pouch drawing shut.

LIFTING SNOW

If you stay in the house long enough,
months after it's over and she's deep
in a new relationship, you will see the
veil between you shimmer and form,
shimmer and fade. Moments as if
everything is as it was before, familiar,
content. She will cheerily call out
"welcome home!" before either of you
remember this is no longer home, and
you have been irrevocably turned away.
Vapors freeze. Snow focuses, floats like a
fine vow. If it were just a flurry, maybe—
But honestly, the ground is already too
frozen to bed the daffodil. The pumpkin
planted in July in a fit of optimism is
stunted, smaller than its pie pan.

Snow That Falls Like Chalk

Once we learned a mathematical proof
that concluded 1 = 0.   What then is
proof? So ran our past and future, filling
the blackboard, chalked faster than we
could copy, dust accumulating in the
trays, drifting, spilling to the floors—
walls of boards chalked with symbols—
hurry, try to understand before—erasing,
refilling. Symbols of something tried and
(succeeded) (failed) (none of the above).
One day we simply walked away.   If a
ghost can sound footfalls, then surely we
were ghosts. A ghost hears itself, but itself
is nothing. 1 = 0. Lonely. Lonely. Lonely.

Snow Soliciting Small Bets,

shuffling, cutting, dealing across the
highway, we cannot see as far as it takes us
to stop for our accident solidifying as we
slide into it, wheels locked up, calf muscles
locked up, our bodies saying, sorry, can't
help you this time, save yourself. Of course
we can't, it's a zero-sum game.

Trickster Snow

This freshly bathed world wrapped in a hotel-white towel, a plain beauty! We no longer remember how shaded she can be, can't feel the green air, can't hear the hubbub of working trees instant messaging. We forgot the pain of ice intimate with our wrists, with our achilles. The pain surprises us with its specific, exquisite press. We forget the exact interval between feeling and feeling.

Snow That Falls Like Amnesia

For the big nouns   Truth Faith Trust Love   all her
images have been stripped   She can't recall everywhere lie
crystalline sundials   She can't recall every   where lies   She
bundles up   goes walking in statistics   disinterest   reversals
Can only think she once thought   beauty   If she   kept
walk   ing kept   walking   kept walk   ing until she   slept a
snow mummy who   when found   would be remembered
only   for being found in snow   perfect   as if   she would
open her eyes and speak   were she not shattered   What
image now   can she claim   This evidence   small animals
tracking among the stones   The field beyond   indicated
by an absence of trees   Or the graves themselves   her new
lake to walk around   the world on her left   death on her
right   or   an image of death   The snow   like a calm hand
stays the clock hands of the dewy dead

Cups

In the china cabinet were six hooks for teacups, eight cups

N-stars: Second Key

Think: skate guards
Prescience, pre-wreckage
The day before the hole reveals itself in clothing
The sound of the cupboard opening
In the house you no longer own
Drifts of the compasses of maps—those N-stars—
Having forsaken their maps

Falling, Falling, Then Rain, Then Snow

Time's sharpened her, me
Edged to a precipice, edged over, edged in,
Falling, falling, then rain, then snow.

I wake in disequilibrium untethered
By left, no north nor theory.
The double helix of her and me unravels,

Years of coils, unruly coils of years.
Some greater genetics codes
The helical arrangement of our souls

Then easily unzips us.
We understood this arrangement
To be physical. Now I am a single strand

Not even I myself can read. I am alerted,
But falter, to replicate a twinning
String of sense but my signals

Will not tune in, elemental
Letters won't hook up, won't
Mean. Nothing means.

HAWKING'S CUP

In Tiwa, the word for soul is *drinker*.

"Disorder increases with time, because we measure time
in the direction in which disorder increases."

—STEPHEN HAWKING

.

We remember the past, and not the future. We know what
is forward and backward in time, as when, in Hawking's
example, we watch a film of a teacup falling to the floor.
When the cup falls from the table to the floor and shatters,
we then know the cup to be broken and we remember it
whole.

When the cup sits on the table in its ordered state, whole,
we remember it whole.

If we were to reverse the arrow of time, that is, if we were
to measure time in the direction that order increases, in the
direction that disordered cups reassemble and leap up to
tables,

—a vestigial meaning of "leap of faith"—

.

then, Hawking argues, we would also reverse the arrow of memory. We would remember the future, not the past. When the cup lay broken, in disorder on the floor, we would remember its future, we would remember it whole.

> (Reversing the direction of motion of all particles defines forgiveness. Buddhists and my dance teacher call this "keeping your death before you.")

•

Chimera's Rabbit

Just outside the entrance to Notre Dame's bell tower, one chimera sits on its haunches, too preoccupied to contemplate Paris. Unlike gargoyles spouting rain and sin, and like nightmares, chimeras are practical only on the soul level. You would recognize this one by his head tilt as he chomps on what he's got both hands around— looks like the legs of a rabbit. His name is Demon Devouring Human Soul. Souvenir statuettes and postcards often portray him, but omit one detail. Unless we lean over the balcony railing, we miss it too: The rabbit is biting back. That prey is claiming her life. Her name is Human Soul Devouring Demon, or, Forgiveness.

CARSON'S WATER

> Question is water is snow,
> Answer is thirst are we.

Anne Carson writes, "a question can travel into an answer as water into thirst." *Question like water, answer like thirst.*

Water travels into thirst, yes, and quenches it, or calms it. So a question, Carson says, satisfies an answer.

Or, if a question pilgrimages to an answer, then water transfigures into thirst.

Meaning sneaks in wearing this cranked-up rhetoric. The hyped-up mystical syntactical meanings mean. *What is* catches like a burr, holds two snatches of cloth close, making a space for itself in the raiment in which there is no space. Until we look here.

JACOB'S LADDERS

Like Jacob, we lay our heads on stones
and fear. Luckily it's all energy and talking
cells. The stones collaborate with our
head bones, shoot filmless film, and we see
the necessary ladders. Ladders, we think,
we must climb. But we should decline
thinking. We wake exhausted and like
Jacob say, "how dreadful." Well, then we
lean our heads on stones and fear. Luckily
it's all energy and talking cells. We're the
star, and the close-up is pretty darn close,
practically behind us. Luckily there is no
here, exactly. One day it might occur to us
to ask what the ladders are made of and
what our answers are made of. Angels, like
Jacob. Or galaxies. Or DNA. Or snow.
Or now, like Buddha. Or teeny tiny tea
parties, like Edith Ann. Everyone gets to
be right and brilliance grows the small love
in fear. In the beginning, the seedlings
look so much alike, two hands waving
stop. Luckily, go is bigger.

Kinds of Snow

Depth of Snow
What one eye sees and the different *what* the other eye
sees are made to focus on one point. "Look, look," is what
we ask of our companions.

Needling Snow
Snow needles
we don't want
touch there
is no breath
to say
enough
breath only
for breath

Butoh Snow
Bright carrots, black coal, and brittle sticks
Lower themselves into the earth
As if into a scalding bath

Snow Harlequin
Blue paper heart.
Tear it in half.
Paste below each eye.

Snow That Stacks Like Vertebrae
We breathe up the front of our spine,
Down the back of our spine.
How little we know our own spines.

Snow, What Is a Dream?
A kite to gall or glide,
A glass to cut or cup.

Snow In Flight
We watch, so many films flashing at once.
We brighten the ponds and rivers below.
We keep our own narratives close.

Striking Snow
The past curtained off,
The scenes struck.
And the future?
We are caught in
Snapping velvet seats
Turning our
Programs over and
Over. The inserts
Have fluttered.
The sloping floor.

COLUMNS

We fell together

THE INCUBUS

Nothing was the same after the incubus.
I had been sleeping, woke with her in me and
Watching. Some winters the cold comes early, deep
And sets in for the duration. Could be years
Before you feel warm. Never again
She said, after the second time.
I stopped sleeping at night, slept at dawn so when
The nightmares came I could wake in the light. Spent
My nights listening to breath, the dogs' and hers.
When hers stopped, I shook her and yelled, "breathe"—why?
It was not a question I could ask then. Once
When it was minus-twenty-something degrees
I went out walking for miles with the intent
To freeze to death. But the body is made to live,
Fiercely. In spite of me, it walked me back to
Our bed while snow was falling, visibility
Poor, I could not see the snow was showing
Me the shape of my life rubbed away

Lullaby

You would love me if?
———— I will love you if and if and when.

You would love me when?
———— I will love you when and when and after.

You would love me after?
———— I will love you after and here after.

You would love me here?
———— I will love you here and here and now.

You would love me now?
———— I will love you now and now and so.

You would love me so?
———— I will love you if when after here now so.
———— I will, I will love you so.

SHIFTING

The sound of shifting
whether it's snow, water, sand, or leaves
is essentially the same cadence
ebb and wane, lift
and settle, gather and abrade.
What pushes behind
wave and particle, patter and koan?

As I wait for you here trying
not to look like I'm waiting for you
here, the sound of shifting
is between us: sh-sh-sh
background, foreground,
opening and wrapping up
many things, one main thing
becoming a new sound, sounding
like the same sound before
of fear, of just the wind
of whimsy, of threat
of prairie and big sky
of urban trees and house eaves
foretelling storms or
foretelling clearance.

If you have questions, it questions;
if you have answers, it confirms;
sensually attentive and disengaged.

The snow of our courtship, crystalline, flashing;
the water we drain, bail, regrade against, redirect;
the sand in our bed, grains of our days
warm layers over cool layers, a desert-full;
the leaves we attempted, August-dry,
false autumn, false-positive;
what pushes behind
wave and particle, patter and koan?
sh-sh-sh
the sound of shifting is between us.

All This I Brought to the End of the Peninsula

. . . she had misunderstood
What she was praying for . . .
The path she'd been on
And the prayer without ceasing
Had led to this:

—DEBORAH KEENAN

Not Franny's prayer but as constant,
Not Keenan's path but the same result,
I was a silver girl with Simon and Garfunkel's

Silver promise: *your time, dreams, etc.,* yet—
Anyone back from the front of betrayal did say—
But then I said, it is never a mistake to love.

Now here I am picking apart arborvitae seeds,
Burdened with promises to the dead,
With memory no one will help carry.

Trungpa advises: lean into the sharp points
But I already know how to burn and heal, bleed
And heal. It's the willow that first releases.

Maybe I confused the word *perfection*
As in, I have perfected the child's lesson on the difficulty
Of taking off a coat without letting go of the sweet.

I'm thinking of Jim Moore's olive trees,
How Jodie Foster in *Contact*, said,
"They should've sent a poet."

I am a poet, and all I've been able to write is
Beautiful. Beautiful world. Yes
But enough.

At the end of the peninsula, I step into the lake.
A young woman, ten-ish, heralded by her beagle,
Announces, *I think I'll join you*

My dream is not to be a writer, my dream is to save
Animals, how much have you written so far?
Blonde, blue eyes, those great in-between teeth,

Some baby, some permanent. White dress,
Everyday, believe it or not.
A lane of light turns toward us.

Did you write about the ducks?
They're coming back from winter—
The weirdest spring I ever had

Began last spring; a man with
Developmental delay asked me,
"Are you okay? Because we can't tell."

Back from the front of betrayal
I can write only three words,
beautiful, yes, enough.

With a startling and contagious ease,
The girl reaches to shake my hand and says,
I hope to see you here again.

PLATES

Like two cups, one nested in the other, that had to be moved whenever a plate was wanted

What Prevails

Though last night's grins were eaten out of pumpkins
And conditions suggested a killing frost,

Some pariahs were embraced. The grief that holds
While it happens is different than the let-go

Grief that in the open doorway encloses.
Unlike law, in love there is no exit.

And pariahs, born to the border life, will
Slip limits. Today it is warm enough

To raise from the neglected litter one
Leaf. Look, it's a monarch. Call her Ruth.

AS PROOF I OFFER EGRET
AND EGRET-IN-THE-WATER

Children drop from playground equipment like ripe apples,
then—gravity's just a slipknot for them—spring back up,
make themselves green again.

All is one, all time is one, and twisting
the stems of apples answers love.

If we keep our deaths before us, we cannot remember
falling—children save their deaths under beds, in closets,
behind sleep. Dogs give quiet guard.

One day the apple children will fall and stay red.
Where is the bottom edge of the sky? It passes through us.
To clouds, we are clouds-in-the-earth.

ICE

The geese were speaking, calling
From the lake, *Don't hold back love.*

Why don't you eat a little something?
One goose's wing was broken.

Hundreds faced the same direction.
The moon was falling on the ice.

The lake closed, then it opened
Like slow breathing.

The Last Of

Summer is leaving my body. I cut
The last of the gold from my hair nine months
After my grandmother reached for it her last

Wakeful day. Summer is leaving. An artist
Gave me a doll, asked me to give the doll
A vagina. Instead I gave her a womb.

I gave her a milkweed pod
Blown open, almost empty of seeds,
One seed on her right, three on her left.

I looked up from my work, the maple was in rapture
I looked up from my work, night had wrapped her
I looked up from my work, the maple had risen

From her leaves, the last of summer, I
Dreamed of sparrows with worn wings and feet,
Not deformed, not broken, worn,

Worn away. The sparrows wanted only
To eat dream creatures. I watched
Summers drain in the mouths of sparrows.

It was early summer the last time, the first time,
Butterflies reached me, devoured me.

Rehearsal for Metamorphosis

The last time I slept in a king-sized bed, I could move,
and move, and still there was bed to hold me.
I did not fall out like I did in our second year—
how many times?—in our single bed,
our bodies learning our bodies, and learning to turn
without traveling. Turning without traveling,
then, and all the years since, all the things I
thought I would do, never thought I would do,
while holding her. Now I am single, again
sleeping in a king-sized bed with all this room,
but I do not move.
I sleep in one narrow tunnel
like a caterpillar in rehearsal.

> We were beautiful like practice paper,
> abandoned sheaves of brief brilliance.
> In this world where beauty is currency,
> even perennials die.
> *If we were to reverse the arrow of time—*

I sleep like an arrow in a quiver. How lonely
was I long before I remembered, now
that I am what I always wished to be: my future
self come to tell me about myself now.
That arrow. This bed. How many more times will I sleep
in a quiver? Turning without traveling.
Then, who nocks me? Readies me? Whose fingers release
me? Who holds in position while I wing?

NEEDLES

What did we do, exactly?

GHOSTI

*Once I have left a cup in the sink to signify that
I am coming back, I shall take my leave*

The last warmth of its body fitted the
snow to the squirrel. Tucked into snow
like packing material, though unpackaged,
the squirrel lies with its left paw resting on
its high, dead heart. There are no tracks,
no umbilical cord; there is no leaving trail.
This snow angel is keeping quite close to
its maker. A perfect cell. So the squirrel
imprinted itself with its weight, not its
warmth, saying, "To claim my soul equity,
I throw myself down, O Death!" Death is
our *ghosti*. With death we have reciprocal
duties of hospitality. Latch bar and
notch, particle and wave. The unknown
is packed like snow and fitted to us. The
squirrel's right paw is frozen as if boxing
the air. At 28 squirrel-lengths east, then
a right angle up to an unknown height,
the air boxes an empty nest. What force
directed the hypotenuse of the squirrel's
fall? Some things will not be made sense
of, and others, the sense we make of them
is false. Squirrels do not remember what
they bury; they make a field of chance.
We make a field of sense and, whether
that has helped us or not, we proceed into
winter, foraging.

Kinds of Ice

Consonants to Call Us
A quick of grackles rush like leaves reversing
Into trees, rattle like pushed ice sharding the shore.

Skating Rink
Geese overhead, single-file, turn, fly back and farther,
Loop south again, tracing the figure of infinity.

The Direction of Our Conveyance
Today renders even the sparrow's breath against—
Not loss—the pull-back currents.

Crossing Over Is the Least Action
A duck barges through border ice, creates canals
Like a child boot-toeing frozen puddles: teeyak, tee, teeyak.

BORDER CODE

I am altered, alerted to transcribe myself.
You, my moon, my sense strand,
This is my replication.

We dream of Escher-escalators,
Staircase drop-offs, rotting ladders.
We dream of tornados.

What border code keeps one, keys one to ice?
What was water yesterday meets what is water yet,
In caresses, harmonics of sparrow song.

PAPER GATE

—as if heaven or the veil were

Arches paper, wet
You, color without purchase
I, muleish, failing brush,
Touch the last of you to it

—my inability to follow you all the way
could be a function of sight

We look at the cloudless sky, and whether our eyes fix or dance, suddenly a burst of birds like a touch of watercolor swells into swallows, dipping and rising. Caught, we watch this arc but the watercolor swallows fall together into one bird, the one bird into a general mark, the mark drains into the dry blue.

DICKINSON'S ARITHMETIC

Borrowed one from, in Subtraction
She is the lending left digit, pierced

DENDRITES

We promised ourselves

━━━

◦┄◦

⬡

✳

Each Individual Can
Make a Difference

AFTER BARBARA RAS

The guide hollered, *if the monarchs don't make it to Mexico*
  this year
they'll become extinct east of the Rockies—
there are so few left in May 2005, NYC,
in the sweating glass butterfly house inside the Museum
of Natural History, I was the only grownup unattached to
  children,
thousands of P.S. kids on fieldtrips—*a record day*—surviving
this year is really important *don't touch don't touch*
the butterflies are really fragile if you touch them
they lose [what?] [fairy dust]
from their wings then they can't fly anymore
no touching—that's touching! No touching!
The guide pulled on my arm with the grip of the drowning
on foam, *where are you from?* Minnesota. *Good*
promise me you'll plant milkweed. As I answered, I thought
I had planted milkweed a few years ago but what comes
up instead are these giant hoary podless flowerless weeds
  when
you touch them they lose stinging slivers in your burning
  skin,
the ones along with the sticks of asters
I bent away from my dog who crawled into the garden to die,
after this, I thought, I am going to hate
the smell of asters forever, but then she was still
living so I thought, no, I will love it. But
I do not love those weeds that are not milkweed, yes

I said to the guard of the butterfly
house I will plant milkweed. Today wound
in a quilt, I am tucked against the big window in the light
of the white sky, two lines in a poem like pus
around a sliver expelled some grief
"of the black dog, the look that says, If I could I would bite
every sorrow until it fled, and when it is August,"
it was too late to plant milkweed. A promise
broken is less than less than dust.

Helix

What impels the reversal, the extrication of stars
From water so that dust to dust may go?

That last day I said, look, leaves are falling
Already. Then a gate unlatched.

That Slider

– enzyme / field / function / god –
signifier –
zips, unzips

nil and tooth –
death and life –
antisense and sense –

a borrowed yes –

that sliding catalyst
is an awful gift of let-go yes

So Cold It Takes Our Breath

AFTER LUCILLE CLIFTON

To speak

We alter

Our breath we

Alter our

Life we

Prolong

The next in

Breath

To speak

We die

A little

Memoir in Snow: A Set of Keys

Keys cut to fit
The wards of my loneliness
And the wards of keys:
Box, bridge, hook,
Sash, solid, wheel
What I can, I say with snow

SCROLLS

We learned a language that some said was unspeakable

HOOKED

Out from under the hard edge
Of her shoulder blade, pain stalked
Her palm like a closed letter,
The kind of letter that, hooked,
We keep but never reread,
With the heaviness of the spent
Hollyhock's spiraling fall.

FROM MY HANDS FALLING WERE FATHOMS

I was Cassandra's audience.
Pain and poverty were pulling a curtain
And something I still cannot mark.

Some injuries are not sudden
But result from repeated
Measures of minor imbalance,
Nicks mouthed by the metronome,
Adding up to an epic of error.

One day the yellow-banded tree felled
Itself. Who knew it had been hollowing?

Arithmetic became abstract
When it was subtracted from the body.
In that craft it is correct to step back
To where everything used to balance and
From the past perfect the present.

Theater remains an art of the imperfect.
It counts on the body and its audience.

I was dancing.
Cassandra was nicking her abacus.
From my hands falling were fathoms.

MANUSCRIPT, ATLAS, THE FIELD

Like a dreaming dog, his hands are running
or typing, or lecturing, tapping the manuscript
in his lap while he sleeps. My body tries
to make itself a private space, folds my legs
up onto the airplane seat, close to fetal.
This old bulldog, part lab, is somebody's sweet grandpa,
somebody's difficult dad, a widower perhaps, alone
with his wedding band. Certainly he is a World
War II vet; even when he moves, something
is always still. He must have been a pilot.
He tracks our flight on a yellowed, dog-eared atlas
that he alternately hides under his manuscript
and reveals to turn the page. British Columbia,
Alberta, Montana, North Dakota, Minnesota.
Like how dogs read earth, focused and loose,
the folds of his skin pour through his trifocals.
Squinting out of his doze as we start to descend,
he hides the manuscript with the atlas, turns
to page 74, "Minneapolis, MN" and rotates it
north, northwest as he reads the snow-dusted landscape of
Pig's Eye Lake, the river bend, I94, the Metrodome.
When I ask if he's from Minneapolis, he says,
"Yes, we're here, here's the field"
and closes his eyes. Now his mouth moves
as if speaking little bubbles of spit, now showing
his teeth like a guarded dog. Sleeping over
a manuscript can look like reading it. If he turned
the page I would think he mastered osmosis,
what we all dreamed of in college. We dreamed
of taking it all in, safe, and unwatched.

On Trying Not to Confuse
Emptiness with Loneliness

Empty mind, empty thoughts
Empty ego, empty pain
Empty shoe (one step at a time)
Empty calendar, plate, tub, bed
Empty pocket, tank, tree, bird
(still clinging to the bough that broke)
Empty word, stage, promise, box
Empty sky, grave, heart, glass
Empty hand, dog, field, gesture
Past, future
Empty, empty try another
Empty house
Empty house
O
Yes
Everything empties itself of you

BEWILDERING SNOW

The salmon rub the crystalline rim to
ringing. Snow settles in the embrace of
each seed pod, each branch and bough.
They hold, everything, even as in white
air geese call change and mourning doves
inevitably lull, let: go, go, go,

Snow That Spills Like Milk

My hands this morning pouring re-
membered how it felt with milk unbal-
ancing inside the carton, the distorting
carton's resonant "dwop," misjudging the
flow, knocking over glasses, milk all over,
scolded "God damn it! Can we have one
meal when nothing spills?" Milk seeping
through the cracks in the table and from
the underside my dog Cokie's tongue
flickering like clouds licking up the light.
Always a disaster. Now I, weary grownup,
imagine night after night of spilled milk.
Would I be able to say instead: you must
have grown since yesterday, something
must have changed inside you, unbalanc-
ing you like milk when you pour—you
haven't yet caught up with yourself. What
if whenever I spilled all the years, I would
have remembered those words "you must
have grown." I looked up this morning
from my hands out to the snow pooling
around this house, pouring down the hill,
all the snow of the past three years, twen-
ty-five years, of my twenties, thirties, for-
ties. *You must have grown.*

Whorling Snow

Dark, dark—even after solstice, clouds
keeping it down, draining like a bath,
draining away what was, revealing an
empty vessel. We know promise. We know
hide and seek. How long do you wait for
it to find you? How long before you push
the moment, dash for what is safe? You
think you're not getting anywhere, but it
isn't where, it's how—you're getting some
how, and you turn, as the snow turns,
dark, dark, along the great spiral.

Kinds of Snow

Sparrow Snow
Snow jumps like sparrows from the middle of the arbor-vitae to its edges, appearing whole out of disappearance. Our eyes are too slow to see the continuity of sparrows. They jump or spring from the bush to the feeder—where does this coil reside in them? Then from the feeder back to the bush. Their language we call song because we do not understand its poetry, its prosody, its litany of kinds of shadows. We take it as a mythology of joy.

Snow of the Fields
The snow of the fields this year is sparse. A tweed of snow, dirt, and corn stubble. Another farm sold. A quick creep of houses.

Snow That Reminds Me of My Mother
This tumble of oranges in the grocery store
in November, she recalls her San Diego
wedding, the orange blossoms

Breaking Snow
Walk with a wider stance, with gravity surely landing each step, with the confidence of a Cooper's hawk pitched at a hundred sparrow wing beats into arborvitae.

Blue Moon Snow

There is snow that comes in bulk and brings silence, because it stops us. This hour we would not otherwise be given, a discontinuity in our industry, a mended film, with many frames missing.

Negative Snow

A mended film, with many frames missing. A leap of faith of narrative, of flight from dark to bright to dark. The shadow overhead returning from the highest tree.

The Snow That Burns in My High Heart, after Sending Sparrows Out of My Body

Our high heart is where our left hand rests when we curl into fetal position. If, as we uncurl, we let our left palm turn over, to press our opening chest, we are now touching ourselves as we do when taken aback. A part of our souls would jump out if we did not hold ourselves there. But gravity's just a slipknot, and souls sometimes send themselves away, home, safe. The shaman retrieves them, blows them back into our high hearts.

Snow of Short Term Memory Loss

Is it snowing? yes.

Is it snowing? yes. It is snowing.

Is it snowing? yes. It is still snowing.

Is it snowing? yes. It snows all day.

Snow That Falls from Books
If you turn the page from the corner, it can sound like walking in snow.

Rising Snow
Snow rises at the heat of the window like joy.

Snow That Reminds of the Dying Dog
We no longer know whose life we are praying for
It is late April and the daffodils are budding

Snow of the Calendar
All the little marks.
Dictators.

The Snow That Attaches,
The snow that falls away.

Other Kinds of Snow
There is snow that falls separate from the sky, and snow that is the sky itself falling, the sky itself reaching down to us (not falling). This is confusing. What does it mean to become lost? Sparrows need carry no marrow, only air. They move easily within this truth. The truth being that brilliance is all there is. The rest we make.

DEPTH HOAR

We laid ourselves down on two lonelinesses

"I want it to be something I will miss," said de Kooning to Rauschenberg, "something really difficult to erase." Rauschenberg had been working with no-image, and he had an idea. So he asked for a drawing from de Kooning and then erased it. Would it help to understand why by seeing it? "No, probably not," said Rauschenberg. Only two people could have looked at this palimpsest and followed the traces back into the richly layered drawing it had been, and now they are both gone. For anyone else, *Erased de Kooning* frames a question and its absence. What was it that de Kooning had loved?

I find an empty envelope, turn it over. "To My Beloved" it says, in familiar handwriting. Tucked in with an old cassette, a note "With love to the angel who came when I called." I experience these documents as curious evidence; wonder what the envelope had held, who was she when she wrote, who was I when I first read *beloved, angel*. All the angels of the past several years include you, Dear Reader. In the multiverse of replicating selves, in this moment, you are the me I have been talking to, the me reading to find the pattern we know is there. Our bodies coded to coherence. *We are the thing itself.* Then why do we calculate decoherence? If we sign angel, our ecstatic fingers unfurl small wings from clavicular concealment. Remember when our pilot left us doubly suspended? He concluded his announcement with only: *and, uh*

GLACIER

You want to hear that I've met someone,
found a good job, bought another house.
You want to hear that I've moved on.
Instead I tell you, I've gone from point A to
point A, no point at all. My dead beloveds
no longer lean in the threshold to watch me
write through the night, no longer do they
stand behind me to supervise my cleaning,
no longer do they amble companionably
around our old lake. Truth, Faith, Trust,
Love. The dead beloveds are quiet now. Yes,
it is lonelier, but what they had observed in
me contented them. Some unknown has
placed its hands in mine. Together we are
a glacier. Fields of snow have fallen away.

The Word Snow

Printing words brings forward dark space,
brings forward what I protect. I light my
wordlessness. That long year I was capable
only of referring you to "The Glass Essay."
If the word is *snow*, it is not the lee of
trees, not the dog lying in the road, not
the architecture of cradling. If the word
is *light*, it derives from snow bringing
forward the world's boundlessness. The
lambent amber moon, curving toward
eclipse, sidelights the river birch and
golden grasses. In this light I walk to the
drift-carved peninsula, onto the ice-glazed
sundial. I remember a girl in white with
her beagle, and I am simply happy, and
numb with snow.

MELTING SNOW

She knows snow by its call name, which
means kin; dogs make snow angels; angels
are defined by absence; she has touched
gates of rapture; bare earth grows at the
heat of trees; the moment arrives when
nothing more can be said; because she
must again let go of something she loves;
because the body both unites and divides
with beauty: The white bowl tilts. Snow
weeps toward equinox. In the kitchen in
a house of healing, a woman is halted,
her measuring spoon poised. The lesser
measures dangle.

NOTES

Firn, prisms, cups, columns, plates, needles, dendrites, scrolls, and depth hoar are some of the classifications of snow.

"A Memoir in Snow: First Key," "N-Stars: Second Key," "Memoir in Snow: A Set of Keys": "A musical key is a song's home," www.dummies.com. "I'll tell you my / dream. Here, here, here be my keys" Shakespeare, *The Merry Wives of Windsor,* Act III, scene 3.

"I can't anymore tell you how it was": *Poseidon Adventure* screenplay by Wendell Mayes and Stirling Silliphant, adapted from the novel by Paul Gallico.

"All for Nothing": For the Haida, salmon mythically represent compassion and transformation. I imagine these salmon encircle us each day, swimming the horizon, sometimes making themselves visible at sunrise and sunset.

"Snow That Falls Like Amnesia": with gratitude to Patricia Weaver Francisco, and to Deborah Keenan for "big nouns" and the snow mummy.

"Hawking's Cup": "the word for soul is drinker," Joseph Rael, *Being and Vibration*. "Disorder increases with time," Stephen Hawking, *The Illustrated A Brief History of Time*.

"Carson's Water": "a question can travel," Anne Carson, "Anthropology of Water" in *Plainwater*.

"All This I Brought to the End of the Peninsula": after Deborah Keenan, title poem of *Willow Room, Green Door*. For Franny's prayer see *Franny and Zooey* by J.D. Salinger; for Jim Moore, see "Olive Trees" in *Lightning at Dinner*. "Bridge Over Troubled Water," lyrics by Paul Simon and Art Garfunkel. *Contact* screenplay by James V. Hart and Michael Goldenberg, adapted from the novel by Carl Sagan.

"As Proof I Offer Egret": "twisting / the stems of apples answers love": To play this old game, hold an apple in one hand and with your other hand, twist the apple's stem. With each twist, say a letter of the alphabet, *a, b, c,* until the stem breaks off. Whichever letter the stem breaks at is the first letter of the name of your true love.

"The Last Of": after Deborah Keenan, *Willow Room, Green Door*; Haley Lasché, "Day of Lament"; and April Sellars' performance art *V*.

"Ghosti": "Once I have left a cup," email from Jane Siberry. "O Death!" Virginia Woolf, *The Waves*.

"Each Individual Can Make a Difference": after Barbara Ras, "You Can't Have It All" in *Bite Every Sorrow*.

"So Cold It Takes Our Breath": after Lucille Clifton, who said at a reading in Minneapolis, "It's life we do not survive."

"On Trying Not to Confuse Emptiness": "Empty, empty try another," Joni Mitchell, "Smokin'."

"de Kooning Snow": *Robert Rauschenberg, Man at Work*, directed by Chris Granlund; *Encounters with Rauschenberg*, by Leo Steinberg.

"Coherence Snow": "only decoherence calculations . . . can tell us when...to treat two terms as non-interacting," Max Tegmark, "The Interpretation of Quantum Mechanics: Many Worlds or Many Words?" "We are the thing itself," Virginia Woolf, "Sketch of the Past" in *Moments of Being*.

"Glacier": thanks to Judith Howard and Katrina Vandenberg.

"The Word Snow": For "The Glass Essay" see *Glass, Irony and God*, by Anne Carson.

ACKNOWLEDGMENTS

I am grateful to the editorial and production teams of the publications in which the following poems first appeared, sometimes in different versions: *Animal Poems* (Red Bird Chapbooks); *Bellingham Review; BLOOM; Body of Evidence; Cuttthroat; Midway Journal; The Normal School; Saint Paul Almanac; Sleet Magazine; Packingtown Review, a publication of the University of Illinois; Poetry City, USA; The Quiet Eye: Thirteen Ways of Looking at Nature; Tinderbox Poetry Journal; Water~Stone Review;* and *White Space Poetry Anthology.*

I am especially grateful to Dede Cummings of Green Writers Press, who shepherded this book with love and joy.

During the 12 years of the making of this book, many people—more than I can name here—supported me. Heartfelt thanks to the Klatch and to Nancy Aarsvold, Sophie Cabot Black, Annie Breitenbucher, Daisy Christopherson, Coco, Jen Connell, Kelly Connole, Sher Demeter, Sierra Dickey, JB Dudley, Michelle Filkins, Connie Ford, Patricia Weaver Francisco, Raelani Greenlee, Holly Harden, Judith Howard, David Hunt, Richard Jarrette, Deborah Keenan, Athena Kildegaard, Laurel Poetry Collective, Anne Lundberg, Maisie, Daniel Martin, the Metropolitan Regional Arts Council, the Monday Poets, Jim Moore, Lewis Mundt, Yvette Nelson, Northfield Arts Guild, David O'Fallon, Kathleen Peirce, Barbara Ras, Spencer Reece, Suzanne River, Jane Rodich, Rosie, Regula Russelle, Shanna Schultz, David Skluzacek, Jim R. Smallen, Jim S. Smallen, Joanne Smallen, Adepeju Solarin, the Southeastern Minnesota Arts Council, Joan Staveley, Robbi Strandemo, Susanna Styve, Michael Tonry, Katrina Vandenberg, Christopher Watson, Jennifer Windsor, Maya Washington, Linda White, my grandparents and their House of Healing, and you, Dear Reader.

CPSIA information can be obtained at www.ICGtesting.com
Printed in the USA
LVOW08s2021071016

507895LV00006B/8/P